THE EVOLUTION OF TAYLOR SWIFT

THE EVOLUTION OF TAYLOR SWIFT

CASSIDY SILVERWOOD

CONTENTS

CHAPTER 1

Disclaimer

The content in this book is intended for informational and entertainment purposes only. While every effort has been made to ensure the accuracy of the information presented, the author and publisher make no representations or warranties of any kind, express or implied, about the completeness, accuracy, reliability, suitability, or availability with respect to the content of this book.

The views and opinions expressed in this book are those of the author and do not necessarily reflect the official policy or position of any individual, company, or organization mentioned. Any resemblance to actual persons, living or dead, or actual events is purely coincidental.

This book is not intended to defame, libel, or slander any person, company, or organization. All references to individuals, companies, products, and brands are for illustrative purposes only, and no affiliation with or endorsement by them is intended or implied.

The author and publisher disclaim any responsibility for any actions or outcomes resulting from the application of information contained in this book. Readers should seek professional advice or conduct their own research when making decisions based on the content provided.

CHAPTER 2

Introduction

This book is an exploration into the career of one of the greatest pop stars of this generation - Taylor Swift. It will look at her career trajectory, touching on her transition to global pop star as well as her beginnings with country music, her impact over the years, and her future musical and professional legacy. Locked inside a world of perfectionism, Taylor succeeded when she dared breach the walls of her fortress of the self; eventually arriving at the door of a collective feeling and finding freedom in her art and expression. This book sheds light on Taylor Swift's journey, and all the excitement and possibility she has kept stowed away in her heart up till now. Hopefully, that melodious freedom resonates with those who seek it.

This book is sectioned to help chart the progression of Taylor Swift's career thus far. "Beginnings" charts the origins of the girl Taylor and the woman that would become Taylor Swift. "In the Key of Country" explores Taylor's literal and figurative roots in the realms of country music, and her inherent status as a storyteller. "Aim for the Pop Star" discovers her rise to power and her expansion in speech and fashion (among other things). "Reputation" and "Folklore" act as mirrors; one brandished sharp and loud and the other soft and quiet where Taylor holds them up to her own heart to discover the truth of herself. "Epilogue" is focused on Taylor's current career transformation and the impact her choices have for the future as contributors to her art and her legacy going forward.

CHAPTER 3

Chapter 1: Taylor Swift's Early Life and Entry int

In this chapter, we delve into Taylor Swift's early life and her introduction to the country music scene. Influenced by her grandmother and introduced to the music of a legend in her own lifetime, Sigourney Weaver, Taylor's musical palette expanded into musical theatre at a young age. As she approached double digits, she was moving to the country, absorbing the music of the south that would later shape her career.

In early 2004, a young Taylor Swift met manager Dan Dymtrow at the Bluebird Café. After the performance, Taylor claims Dymtrow gave her his card and called her daily, but ultimately nothing came of the offer. However, as the cards folded and the calls faded, another producer found interest in the starlet. As the Swifts were preparing to relocate to Nashville, The Highwaymen's Robert Orr extended an invitation for Taylor to work with them. Although three of the four record labels initially rejected the idea of Taylor Swift, Scott Borchetta saw potential in the young artist. In late 2005, at the ripe age of sixteen, Taylor left her hometown behind to move to Nashville and work with some of the best in the industry at BNA Records. In March 2006, her self-titled debut album hit the shelves, bringing her in direct competition with her MySpace fans. It wasn't long before country music fans across the country caught Swift fever. Sponsoring her senior year of high school, she sang four tracks on the 2006 Rascal Flatts tour. She had officially gone from nobody to somebody in a matter of months.

Childhood and Musical Influences

Contrary to the tumult that characterized her teen years, Taylor Swift's childhood was fairly tranquil. Born on December 13, 1989 in Reading, Pennsylvania, music was a fundamental element in the lives of her parents, Andrea and Scott Swift. They sang on holidays, and the house was always soaked with music from the likes of Bruce Springsteen, Dolly Parton, and Shania Twain. Subsequently, in the car, Tay was introduced to the music of Faith Hill, George Strait, and Garth Brooks by her grandfather, who was an opera singer. Tay and her brother, Austin, grew up admiring their parents' love story and both discovered solace and delight in their art.

Taylor Swift auditioned and was cast as the lead character in a Community Theatre production when she was nine. In Nashville, Tennessee, she found serendipity. Her passion and ambition grew as she began auditioning for commercials and made three trips to Music Row in Nashville. Despite the homesickness and despair that singed her young heart, Taylor remained undaunted and merry. Scott Borchetta and the Big Machine Label purchased her swallow of 12-minute masterpieces when she was 14. "When you put creative minds in a room with the purpose of altering the fact that something is discouraging you, you frequently wind up creating something beautiful that resonates with the masses," Taylor Swift said. She has attended over thirty artists and co-owned red-carpet events across three nations. Her parents were ecstatic when they arrived.

Breakthrough in Country Music

An instant success, her album also spent 24 non-consecutive weeks at number one on the Billboard Top Country Albums Charts. To date, it holds the record for the longest-running album at the top spot since 2006, when her second number one album, 'Fearless' (2008), was released. It also debuted at number one on the famous Billboard 200, which lists the most popular albums in the entire music industry with all genres combined. In her career, Swift would spend the most weeks on this particular list. Furthermore, 'Taylor Swift' was also the top-selling album of 2008. In 2009, she won the Country Music Association Award for Horizon Artist of the Year, and in 2007, she received the Country Music Association Horizon New Artist Award.

She was beginning her journey to worldwide fame. By 2006, Swift had released her first single, also titled "Tim McGraw" after the country singer, with whom she would later forge a personal and professional relationship. In her early years, Swift played in almost-empty bars and coffee shops up and down the East Coast, trying to break onto the music scene. So what happened to change her from that "little girl with the guitar" to one of the best-selling female music artists of the 21st century? One reason is certainly her songwriting talent. Having gained experience in musical theater and talent competitions, she has been writing since she was 12 years old. Furthermore, the personal stories and feelings in the songs on 'Taylor Swift' captured the hearts of her teenage audience and the wider country music community, starting a new trend in country music of relating to a younger demographic of fans.

CHAPTER 4

Chapter 2: Transition to Pop and Mainstream Succes

In the fall of 2014, Taylor Swift reinvented her music, as well as her image, to best position herself to dominate the pop industry. As she embraced the pop genre, Swift worked closely with pop producers and teamed up with Max Martin to pen her first pop single, "Shake it Off". Martin, the reigning king of the pop industry at the time, had been the mastermind behind an impressive thirty-one number one singles before collaborating with Swift to write "Shake it Off". While working on her new album, Swift also sought the advice of Lena Dunham, who she credits with encouraging her to embrace being strong, confident, and independent. As she sought to transform her music and image, Swift also removed her music from the free streaming service Spotify and entered the courtroom to challenge former Denver radio DJ David Mueller when he inappropriately touched her during a fan photo opportunity. These actions of seeking legal recourse and demanding monetary compensation for the damage suffered signify to many that she had reached a new phase of feminism, counter to the fourth wave of feminism against her. The "Shake it Off" music video set the tone for Swift's transition from country singer to pop star by including the generic conventions of music videos from a variety of groups, including ballet dancers, hip-hop dancers, and music superstar Madonna's recognizable "exposing" scene.

The major shift in Swift's musical genre, image, and controversy at the end of summer 2014 concluded a phase of her career and defined this transition as a critical moment within her personal and professional trajectory. This bold move transformed her into a mainstream pop superstar. While fans attempted to acclimate themselves to Swift's new persona after the release of "Shake it Off" in August 2014, they also pushed her pop song to the top of the music charts. In fact, "Shake it Off" became Swift's last number one hit of 2014 and just one of fifteen singles by her to reach the top of the charts.

Musical Shifts and Evolution of Style

Upon her arrival to the pop music scene, Swift's sound underwent noticeable shifts. Reflective of pop-rock and pop-punk styles, her first venture into popular music marked an effort to maintain her love for her teenage years by appealing to her quickly aging audience. Incorporating a heavy focus on relationships, the narratives contained within her lyrics offer a sense of innocence and wide-eyed hopefulness. Since these initial compositions, Swift's approach to songwriting has matured significantly. Subject matter has shifted from self-expression to inspiration and emotional connection. Lyrically, the industry veteran now offers up a lyrical product rich in metaphor and connected to a contemporary audience. Through her narrative, it is argued that Swift's decision to shift her sound was a business-related effort to keep up with her rapidly aging audience.

Perhaps the most obvious change in Swift's evolution has been her style. Her first album, entitled Taylor Swift, is classified as mainstream country. The musician toured heavily throughout various arenas to promote it. Known for performing with her guitar and singing with a southern drawl, Swift used strategically placed glances and quick, exaggerated facial movements to engage a younger audience. With an increasing focus on capturing a mainstream audience, Swift's style evolved through the years. From 2009 to the present, Swift's country wardrobe and microphone remain the same, though arena size and audience demographic have shifted. It is claimed that her age is playing a strong role in how Swift chooses to present herself in the public sphere.

Critical and Commercial Success of Pop Albums

Following the transition from country to pop, this section looks at the critical and commercial success of her pop albums as an established singer-songwriter in pop music. "1989" set new records, received overwhelmingly positive reviews, and further established Swift as an iconic figure outside of country music. Her return with "reputation" provided insights into her lower public profile, facing up to her public persona. "Me!" and "You Need to Calm Down" marked a recreation of the singer herself. "Lover" marked a return to a more laidback, romantic aesthetic following an album that dominated the mainstream discourse. "Folklore" and "Evermore" marked another move away from star persona building and towards focusing on her songwriting and storytelling. Released during the COVID-19 pandemic, Swift would spend time rewriting and rewriting these albums with Aaron Dessner of The National and Jack Antonoff. "Folklore" in particular was a critically acclaimed surprise release that subverted expectations for the pop star; it was awarded the Grammy for Album of the Year in 2021.

Critical and commercial success of pop albums. Leaving her roots behind to enter an oversubscribed genre of pop music was a risk. Swift had already established a star persona in country music, which positioned her as 'relatable, self-reliant, and fundamentally good' - traits that critics believed to be familiar in the genre. Swift says of turning to pop: "I was so tired of seeing people win things and like being so cute. I'm such a softening of their persona, their personality is such a factor in the good things that happen to them. It's like personality is the reason for the win." Having rounded up her country image with the critically acclaimed and commercially plausible "Red," Swift told the world she was no longer country, but pop. The process of making this album, Taylor "felt territorial about it." She said, "For the first time, I realized why people let this get to their heads. I felt somewhat of a starving man – you let a starving man the first meal he's had in forever and the idea of someone noticing you? It's like, I would immediately be like 'really? You think so? D'ya think? Watch this.'" Taylor might have been the one to leave country, but country in general was not willing to let her go. In Australia, "1989" topped the charts for eight weeks. In the US, however, the single "Shake It Off" was capable of but a two-week stay at number one on the charts. It was released at an unfortunate time to face competition from "The Voice" and a new breakout rap hit by Nicki Minaj. The album sold about 1.3 million copies in its first week, making it the best-selling album of 2014. Ultimately, it became her best-selling album, at least physically, and the best-selling album of 2014 in general. The following singles "Blank Space," "Style," "Bad Blood," and "Wildest Dreams" all charted within the top ten of the Billboard Hot 100 in America. The former was her second number one single from the album, a first in her career. It was love that would lift Taylor up, gets on the road that would keep him there." In Australia, "1989" accumulated Platinum certification upon release. In America, the Recording Industry Association (RIAA) was swamped by fans who purchased a similar fate and certified it Platinum in just one week. In 2015, "1989" went one better and went sextuple platinum. On 31st October 2019, the RIAA re-certified the record and, in meeting Sam's record, "1989" was designated as a non-single release; it is now a six-time platinum record. "1989" was nominated for a Grammy for Album of the Year; she won for Best Pop Vocal Album.

CHAPTER 5

Chapter 3: Taylor Swift as a Songwriter and Perfor

In this chapter, the section-key role of Taylor Swift will be scrutinized: her songwriting, her recording, and her performing. This chapter will show that her professional career from 2006 until now is characterized by the continuous recording and performing of her own songs. As a songwriter, Swift unveils a lot of personal matters, which means that in this chapter the themes of her songs will be analyzed as well. Furthermore, Swift's live performances and concert tours will be scrutinized, since these are the periodic highlights in her still short but very productive career. The concert venues are also analyzed, giving a brief overview of the different kinds of concerts Taylor gave per studio album.

One of Swift's main strengths is her autobiographical songwriting, which means that in this chapter her creative process and themes are scrutinized. Besides autobiographical writing, Swift also regularly writes songs based on other people's stories and emotions, which is also discussed. Over the years, Taylor Swift's songwriting subtly adapted to her growing age. Her songs have not only become more mature but her way of writing changed as well. In the very first songs that she wrote when she was still a young teenager, mostly present a responsible and caring image of the little daughter that she would like to be. Taylor more or less describes an idealized version of herself. Concerning the style of her writing, the autobiography of the earliest songs differs from her later work. The in love, and often romantically broken-hearted young girl was present from the beginning and she is also still present in Taylor's songs today. However, the way that she presents herself evolved. Rather than presenting herself in an ideal form, Swift started to present herself as quite the opposite.

Songwriting Process and Themes in Her Music

Taylor Swift's songwriting process and style have been chronicled over more than a decade of interviews, but the most reliable accounts of her process come directly from Swift herself. At an after-show chat in September 2019, Swift explained that she typically starts with small ideas: a melody that pops into her head or a poetic or clever lyric that she jots down. She might air her ideas in the company of her co-writers to see if there is excitement in the room. If not, she moves on to her next catchy idea. This adage guides her process: "We're only interested in getting to a song if we can get to it in the most fascinating way for us." When she's working through a configuration or revising her lyrics, Swift might apply strategies that she learned from her English studies during her freshman year at the University of Pennsylvania. She enjoys writing humor and entendre into her lyrics and is infamous for her easter eggs, references to outside elements, that pop up everywhere from her music all the way to her social media posts. Her diaristic lyrics—often weaving candidly personal topics with coded references to the public figures and industry professionals that her fans have come to know—maintain the intimacy and narrative qualities that drew the audience in back during her country music phase.

The universal themes that she has leaned into began to gain her audience an entry point within the stories by 2008, which helped secure her first top-40 hit when "Love Story" crossed into the pop radio genre stratosphere. Love stories and romantic heartache and recreational "tea spilling" of people who've hurt her have been tropes of her recorded material as well as the narratives that Swift brings to life in her catchy, incisive, and often self-deprecating lyrics. Her lyrical detail has been well-regarded as a talent that Swift has cultivated that makes the stories in her songs "belong to listeners now," according to Bon Appétit writer Alex Beggs. These details, narrated as children's and young adult fantasy stories, circulate Swift's feminism that "belies pop-country-girl stereotypes" and imagines female relationships without competition and distrust and replaces it with warmth and healing. The same critics might balk at the 2017 release of Swift's solo-written "reputation" album, only to be awash in forgiveness for "Lover" in 2019.

Indeed, it's the sharpness of her pop-cultural literacy and the evolving of her own understanding and acknowledgment for the long personal journey to self-worth that makes her narrative compelling. In her "music of the spheres"—as she releases "Red (Taylor's Version)" and rolls 30 songs from "Red" to "Fearless (TV)" to "Speak Now (TV)" onto the Billboard 100—the sociopolitical power of narrative and the panoptic power of memoir that amp listeners on—with alarm, with sympathy, with nostalgia—along with Swift herself. Every person on that path with her sees themselves and feels seen in her songs. From a heavy, blanketed dorm room with a guitar to the cloudless skies of stadia, Swift has always been connecting the dots in life as well as the radio for her listeners to her experiences with these same milestones. Swift has looked critically at her past work and weighed its emotional payload as her audience wrestles with their memories, too.

Live Performances and Concert Tours

Taylor Swift has earned more than two dozen awards for live performances. Critics have nicknamed her concert tours as "shows that raise the stakes and promise whole new worlds." Her dome-sized hook made me dance through her 'Fearless' album that I don't even have, highlighting the narrative expectations that prospective fans and critics arrive with at her tour performances. Her stadium shows combine multiple forms of immersivity. Along with spectacle, she combines hooks, dance, and storytelling into crowd-based sing-along and digital cartography. Taylor Swift's audio and video spectacle tends toward immersive seas of relatively few radiant colors.

These performances exemplify the ways in which stars like Swift turn the stages of transcendence into immersive worlds. Swift's global fan base can connect with her visible, felt presence. Massive screens also ensure that fans can see Swift up-close. The spectacle of Swift's performances is primarily an auditory riot of live vocals, backing tracks, dancers, and ear-aching sing-along harmony carried by concert-goers and Swift herself. In some cases, special effects serve to accent the concert's narrative spectacle. Concertgoers can expect jets of smoke or fire for "I Did Something Bad." These help enact the conciliatory noise of Swift's pre-choruses, creating an experience of pop-worldly agentic affirmation that includes those in the audience. Filmed intimate audio-visceral and personal spectacle put fans into Swift's productively precarious fanarchy of authenticating their just-like-Taylor pleasures. Arena floor wristbands that light up and change in time with the performance create "a glow stick that never falls to the ground of a dark, Chris." Swift also invites fans onstage to meet her during her concerts.

CHAPTER 6

Chapter 4: Taylor Swift's Impact on the Music Indu

Throughout this book, I examine Taylor Swift's profound effect on pop music. In doing this, I trace how she has not only influenced numerous other artists but also introduced her own set of trends from which those artists might draw influence. While Taylor Swift clearly inspires greatly in the musical world, I boldly argue that her influence on individual artists may be dwarfed by the profound effect she has had in shaping the sounds that are emerging in pop music. The days of Auto-Tune and synths calling the shots in pop music are slowly fading away, replaced by an interest in being raw and authentic. By diverging away from the current trends and emerging on her own, Taylor Swift has unknowingly been leading the charge of a sonic war on that takeover, transforming entire genres and leading them into an open world of new growth.

Taylor Swift is a fearless leader in music, but this courage does not exist independent of her other forms of influence. Over the past few years, Taylor Swift has also used her platform to enter social and political activism, from asserting her dominance over her former label by re-recording her masters to leading legal battles and trying to sway public opinion on voting day. DeadSet is a company that now specializes in defining how influence works, but what has happened here when looking at Taylor Swift? She is no longer simply a country star or pop song writer; she is an icon. YouTuber Savannah Marie describes Swift as simply 'indie.' Yes, she is the 'pop princess', but in the end, she is in a class of her own crafting 'mainstream indie' as well. This transition from country star to indie world market influence boasts the clash between the country and indie world, showing that Taylor Swift's style stretches far greater than that of a simple country hit.

Influence on Other Artists and Emerging Trends

Swift's evolution from country star to global icon has provided a roadmap for other artists and has resulted in emerging trends in the current music industry. Swift's business savvy has led her to cultivate a crew of dedicated fans, a group comprised of diverse ages, races, and genders, who are willing to follow her every creative decision. The feel-good emotional messages in her music serve as a connection point for all of her fans across the world, which they feel when listening to her songs. 48 different records of which were bought within the first day of Swift's Fearless tour in 2009. Similarly, underappreciated artists gain guidance from Swift with regards to taking control of their artistry and negotiations. Swift's move to re-record her albums was inspired by a fan's question, but in doing so, she has garnered respect from young, emerging artists facing similar threats of exploitation by record labels that Swift herself has endured.

Music streaming services such as Spotify and Apple Music are facing a trend towards fan backlash when access to a high-profile artist's catalog is temporarily limited. For instance, Taylor Swift removed her music catalog from Spotify in 2014 after arguing that music should not be free. Set in motion when Scott Borchetta sold Big Machine Label Group and related assets, Swift is in the process of re-recording her original masters because she did not have sufficient money to buy them back by the time she left Big Machine in 2019. In purchasing the Big Machine family of records, Ithaca Holdings' acquisition of Swift's music from 2006 to 2017 is a desired move in the country and pop music industry. Music Row noted that the acquisition will "likely strengthen Swift's legacy." A July 2020 lawsuit accuses Swift (or at least her record label) of copying lyrics from an earlier song by Jessie Braham. Notably, the lawsuit comes at a time when Swift has won awards for songwriting, attributing to the fact that she is the only artist to win the award three times.

Social and Political Activism

Beyond her music, the conversations about Taylor Swift have been impacted heavily by her social and political beliefs. Perhaps the first time her position on social issues made international headlines was when Swift, known for her sharp-witted pen in her lyrics, penned a Wall Street Journal article, "For Taylor Swift, the Future of Music is a Love Story" in 2014. She has since publicly endorsed many policies and politicians, though her endorsements are predominantly within her home state of Tennessee.

That being said, there is a large amount of scholarship dedicated to Swift because, unlike many pop musicians, Swift actively seeks out more influence than just her music. She is open with her fans about her life and has rebranded herself more frequently than she has put out new music. This, according to Graham St. John, is an example of the "intensification of the public persona". In these instances, Swift makes herself a subject of public discourse, stepping "out in public, into the arena of concerned others, as a player with a stake, putting herself at stake in the encounter" (St. John 235). In other words, Taylor Swift has proven, through sales and social influence, to gain new fans, and new audiences, with nearly each new image. And her songs, covering personal topics such as love, heartbreak, and new beginnings, reflect these changes (Perone 51). It is important to study her in the decades surrounding her birth because she has the privilege of not only living through them, but coloring directly with her own image.

Chapter 5: Taylor Swift's Business Ventures and Br

Taylor Swift is not only a flourishing entertainment industry professional, but also a successful businessperson. She has proven to be a savvy entrepreneur with investments in various fields including natural health supplements and real estate. Swift has developed a strategic investment approach that involves planting small financial stakes in a variety of businesses related to her interests. This diversified approach spreads her risk. Also, she invests in businesses that promote the issue of good health, something that she promotes on her live tours and in her books. Not content with generic endorsement deals, Taylor has worked directly with brands to co-create new lines for her fans.

Taylor and Capital One Visa teamed up during her 1989 World Tour for exclusive card member pre-sale tickets as well as receiving a financial incentive for the association. In 2018, Swift forged a partnership with Glu Mobile, a mobile game development company. They are the company responsible for making Kim Kardashian's app, which Taylor has the opportunity to play against herself. Also, in 2019, the entertainer co-created two lines of interior painting with popular brand Urban Outfitters and earned an official title from the company. Swift's latest endorsement endeavors include the beer industry where she partnered with Stella Artois for their 'The Places I've Been' campaign. Each of Capital One, Glu Mobile, Urban Outfitters, and Stella Artois was attracted to Taylor Swift due to her standing in her field and the tendency for her fans to be attracted to brands that she aligns herself with. Sincerity, genuineness, altruism, and plain old being nice. Brand manager Anders Stahl also praised the association, saying "we are excited to offer Taylor's fans more access to create their very own co-branded card. We have invested in these areas to reach a younger and potentially more hip customer - and it's working."

Entrepreneurial Ventures and Investments

Aside from her music, Taylor will additionally be making money in a variety of ways. Her net worth is believed to be real estate value in the range of million, in addition to her successful career. The majority of her investments come in the form of business property, especially real estate. In 22 states, she is said to have eleven residential properties, distributed over 35,000 acres. She owns roughly and swiftly spends a combined income of annually on these possessions. On top of the many structures used for permanent lodging and maintenance, Taylor has many Beautiful Houses in different places. She spent million purchasing an Upper East Side townhouse with an impressive array of properties such as beautiful houses, estates, and mansions in numerous locales. Taylor's investment in her music is also a good one to make a profit.

She has, however, proven to be a shrewd entrepreneur even in areas unrelated to her music. Her perfume sales have soared to million in 2021, and she has invested million in a business. In 1949, Taylor bought the eight-bedroom beachfront house with approximately

12,604 square feet of living space on a 4.5-acre lot in an off-market deal. She also makes a lot of money from endorsements. She has worked as a spokesperson for many brands, including corporations in Japan, Verizon Wireless, L.E.I. Jeans, and others. Last year, merchandise sales increased by nearly percent. This year, she will be featured in a fashion spread for Random Fashions's Fall campaign.

Brand Partnerships and Endorsements

Forging a successful advertising and brand-building partnership requires trial and error on both sides. Generally, the more a celebrity fits with a brand's target markets, positioning, and objectives, the better the relationship will be. Swift has long been known for her commercial endorsements, but unusually for a pop singer, many of her series of partnerships revolve around the use of an artist's music. Swift's brand partnerships revolved mostly around the release of her album 1989, in addition to capitalizing on a general cultural moment of either a new album or single release, mostly around athletic endorsements or products in the music streaming and delivery service space itself, the point where she is likely to want product placement on several digital, music and technology-based promotional content platforms, in addition to digital and streaming products as well as physical products and athletic as a brand-whisperer of the health and beauty products she herself is connected.

When a consumer buys a product that Taylor Swift endorses, they are receiving more than just a physical product. The audience buys Swift's highly developed brand, which compliments products of clean, pure, beautiful, and characteristically tailored personal values she has. In a similar way to promotional content and advertising representing Swift first, this segment will have physical products in addition to digital, music and technology-endorsed products. Swift endorses a multitude of products and causes, though her event sponsorships revolve around music products (presumably leading into album releases) and athletic endorsements, her partners reflect her brand, values, and the lifestyle she would like to promote. Apart, Swift has pledged $1m to a charitable fund in support of people who were affected. Her work with the private company "demonstrates how continuous, income-aligned relationships between corporations and artists are often a major component of a constructive celebrity endorsement deal."

CHAPTER 8

Chapter 6: Taylor Swift's Global Reach and Fanbase

Taylor Swift has experienced huge commercial success on an international level, and as such, has developed a large global fan base. Her song "Shake It Off" was the first single to top the charts in the United Kingdom while bagging the second spot in Australia where the "multi-culture motif of 'Shake It Off'" resonated with Australian society, and the song was her highest charting single in France and Germany. Swift's foreign appeal is due to her ability to "mock entertainment culture [through parody] while simultaneously creating an entertaining pop song" and thus believe that "[the] tone of rejection within a transnational hit [like 'Shake It Off'] doubtlessly contributed to its multi-cultural appeal". Moreover, Taylor Swift's music aims to be universally accessible by referencing everyday values" and therefore "represents a culture which is not specifically American, but increasingly a mass culture for everybody".

In addition to her commercial success in Europe, Aleta Lederow asserts that "Taylor Swift directly addresses her fans through her use of social media, and her cursory mentions of her world tours suggest the wide range of her international fan base". Swift's global fan base is exemplified by the world's reaction to her record label court case in 2019, where Swift's fans in Japan and Brazil used the hashtag #WeStandWithTaylor on Instagram to unite with United States fans. Swift has also sparked marketing collaborations with brands in China, which has developed a significant fan base, further confirming her impact on a global scale. Swift's image and music itself have been praised by those in the music and film industries for its international appeal. Music video producer Joseph Kahn claims "If [Taylor Swift] had a different image, a different sound – if she had pink hair and dressed like Lady Gaga – then I think it would be tougher for her to have that kind of worldwide appeal because that is a very western visual [style]".

International Success and Collaborations

The American Music Awards and Billboard named Taylor Swift the first artist of the year, making her the most awarded artist of the two reward organizations. With Taylor Swift being a world-famous singer, more than 100 songs and albums have been certified Platinum and Gold. Logical and highly explicit lyrics, including the topic or song theme, often based on her life, have made this girl more than just a singer. Proof of Taylor Swift's success is that international awards have recognized her. In addition, for the past three years, Taylor Swift's face has appeared on American and British magazines. The high impact has been her five years on the Japanese magazine cover, proving that she has embraced the Japanese and is a global icon.

Taylor Swift admitted she loves Japan and the Japanese people. Every time she comes to Japan, she must watch Japanese films and theater performances. She loves Japanese food, especially sushi. The fourth studio album, Red, which was released on October 22, 2012, was released in 93 countries. This is Swift's biggest album launch worldwide. The album has a single, "We Are Never Ever Getting Back Together", which debuted at No. 1, selling 623,000 copies in the first week. "We Are Never Ever Getting Back Together" is the first song of the album "Red" that any artist who has topped the Billboard and iTunes music charts around the world and has surpassed 2 million sales in the first month of release. A further two singles also saw commercial success, which made Swift a world of fans. By 2013, her albums were considered popular because of the number of albums sold worldwide. In return, this is the recognition of other musicians that Swift is an inspirational musician. It is recorded for 6 days and has 3 versions, including a live version. Furthermore, the album won a Grammy Award for Best Music Video, becoming the first in her career.

Fan Engagement and Social Media Presence

Since her beginnings in 2006 as a country singer, Taylor Swift has been able to sustain a massive fanbase throughout her crossover to pop music from 2012. Building strong relationships with her fans, she is known for such efforts as hosting Secret Sessions at her homes, selecting fans to invite to sound checks, holding post-show meet and greets with Club Red, a youth-oriented Instagram page, and doing various events with outside companies. Additionally, much of the interest on her social media networks is built off interactions, retweeting, and hosting streaming sessions. At one point, Swift hosted a weekly event while she was dating Calvin Harris where her fans could watch her two cats, Owen and Meredith, through Periscope. The intense relationship between Swift and her fans, specifically on Instagram, indicates that across all of her social media platforms, her massive follower count is consistently engaging with her posts. She interacts with fans on many occasions, and reblogs and retweets influence tactics, as well as just making her followers feel significant and noticed.

Her fans are typically referred to as the "Taylor" community in China. This name was selected by Chinese fans in 2018 to exclude the exonym of Swifties. This indicates that the "Taylor" community is homegrown and run by predominantly Chinese fans, chipping away at the idea that the world functions in English. In response to the coronavirus outbreak, Taylor began hosting a singing competition for her Chinese-speaking fans under the hashtag #WeAreFamily, as the Chinese Government locked down Wuhan on January 23. The competition called for any and all fans of Swift who knew the words to "Shake It Off" and could prove themselves musically inclined enough to perform it in some capacity. The contest, titled "Taylor Meets", was held over Twitter and Weibo, awarded 100 prizes, and sported various "landmark" mentions for international outreach on platforms such as Forbes and BBC.

CHAPTER 9

Chapter 7: Taylor Swift's Awards and Achievements

The massive list of awards or accolades that Taylor has earned could and did fill a whole book, or two, or more. Nonetheless, the most prestigious awards that Taylor has collected are Grammy Awards. Since 2008, reasonable people could argue that some of the Recording Academy members had been far from Taylor's side, or liked some of her friends far more, or owned ears impermeable to pop music. Still, Taylor was never left out in the cold, beyond the pale entirely. The only trio of albums that did not win Album of The Year also only has nine, four, and two nominations, which allowed Taylor to earn an "A" on her report card receiving not more than two "albums out" and only one "less nomination" alongside seven "nominations".

The Country Music Association (CMA) also handed out 36 CMA Awards, which could potentially indicate that Taylor is a creature of fortune. Alternatively, it could possibly demonstrate that she has truly made some valuable contributions to country music, and is, at long last, finally being properly acknowledged. The Country Music Association had given her 33 CMA Award nominations throughout her brief career, completing her Indiana Jones franchise quest for country music's golden treasure (popularity and critical acclaim) when she was asked to join the Opry late last year. Shania Twain is the only other woman in country music history to receive as many CMA nominations.

Grammy Awards and Other Accolades

As of December 2021, she has received 38 Grammy nominations and has won 12. With the release of her album Fearless (Taylor's Version), Swift broke the long-held record for most-streamed pop album in a single day on Spotify, with 48 million global streams, and by mid-year 2021, she had broken yet another: she became the first woman in history to debut atop both the Billboard Hot 100 and Billboard 200 charts in the same week – with "Cardigan" and its parent album, Folklore. Additionally, Swift has 14 Guinness World Records and, as of April 2016, with sales of 32 million according to Nielsen SoundScan, was the best-selling digital music artist of all time.

Her other industry awards include: 10 Grammys, the most of any female artist in history; 2 Brit Awards, including the best-selling international artist in the UK for two years in a row; and 11 Country Music Association Awards, including the Pinnacle Award, a special honor voted on by fans and presented in recognition of her impact on country music, according to NBC News. Swift's accolades not only clearly solidify her enormous talent and influence but in the words of the BBC, also illustrate her popularity across the entire music industry. Her following is so strong that she won a 2021 BRIT Award for global icon. According to O2, which is the sponsor of the BRIT Awards, the winner of a global icon award has to have made a "lasting impact on the music industry and [inspired] people from across the world."

Record-Breaking Achievements

Swift's achievements do not lie only within the realm of music but also in terms of her economic success. During her Red era, Swift performed a residency at London's O2 Arena grossing the highest amount of £23.6m, which was estimated to be spent in Old London. Swift has the record for most viewed music video by a female artist in 24 hours with Me!, breaking Adele's Hello (2015) then later her own record. Me!, a brand new song with no preceding promotion, managed to get the record. This was the second time of breaking the record for most viewed video in 24 hours. Shortly after Taylor broke her record of the most viewed video in 24 hours with a new record of 65 mil views in its opening 24 hours, the video was then viewed by 1 mill per hour for the next 8 days. Not for 8 days consecutively but in a total of 8 days will still on the platform and was the only music video to hit a billion views in 9 days. Taylor is the first ever artist to gain over 1 billion global audio streaming in its first week of release, with 1.1 billion of her 1.7 billion audio streams being international, her biggest international streaming audience to date. As well as her album reputation, with 1.055 bill of her 1.216 billion album streams being international.

In modern pop, top ten singles debut with large figures which fail to amount to much, quickly falling after a chart life of approximately eight weeks. It is a very hard period for an artist to achieve upwards mobility with their singles. Swift's first top ten pop airplay debut blank space, which debuted at number twenty-four, took ten weeks to rise from the top fifteen, taking eleven weeks to enter the top ten. The standard chart climb of one to ten has significantly lengthened in terms of the airplay chart, however, recently singles are reaching the top ten much quicker than say five years ago. Blank space took eleven weeks to go from fifteen to one and it was Swift's eighteenth week on the chart when she was at the pinnacle position.

CHAPTER 10

Chapter 8: Taylor Swift's Personal Life and Philan

To this part, Swift has written songs about the following men she dated or was rumored to have dated: 1. Joe Jonas: Forever & Always, 2. Taylor Lautner: Back to December, 3. John Mayer: Dear John, 4. Jake Gyllenhaal: All Too Well, 5. Harry Styles: Style, I Knew You Were Trouble, Two Ghosts, Out of the Woods, Sheeran, Don't. Where possible, she has been able to keep her relationship more private such as Alwyn. Swift's family, however, is another personal story. She is very close to her parents, Scott and Andrea, and her brother, Austin, and likes to bring them on the stage with her at awards shows and on tour. According to the "Daily Mail" in April 2010, Taylor Swift topped the list of the twenty richest young under thirty in the UK and Ireland.

An installment of "Taylor Swift: American Beauty" would be remiss without a chapter on her philanthropy. In her recent Vogue articles, held annually since 2012, Swift has been candid about her giving and what causes are important to her. From 2010 to 2011, Swift donated all of her merchandising profit from her "Speak Now" worldwide tour to charity. In a single year, Swift also gave away one million books to libraries across the country in an effort to introduce children to reading. Some of the organizations Swift has given to include: Big Brothers Big Sisters of Greater Los Angeles; the Cedars-Sinai Medical Center; the Childhood Cancer Foundation in Greece; Country Music Hall of Fame; Feeding America; Habitat For Humanity; the Nashville Symphony and Museum; Nick's Kids; the Reading Foundation; and the Women's Center. In addition to her philanthropy, Swift has won many awards that recognize her as someone who gives back.

Relationships and Public Image

Taylor Swift is known as much for her public image as her music, often for the relationships she has. For many of her early fans, they grew up with songs that progressively got darker and sarcastic songs about seemingly relatable relationships: high school and college relationships or summer romances that drift off. The situation was complicated as Swift began dating famous people. A lot of Swift's professional success is rooted firmly in her public image and the idea of creating connections with her fans. As the idea of fandom has evolved, and the market (especially pop music market) has become utterly saturated, Swift's public image is more than just a part of her music career, she has gotten to play a large part in defining what has become an essential element of the careers of those who came after. Furthermore, Swift has found a home in a public that perceives her, most recently, as the victim of public war.

It is not inaccurate to say that the public knows much about Taylor Swift's personal relationships. She has dated stars from nearly every industry ranging from outside of entertainment to her current boyfriend, a British actor from the Marvel Cinematic Universe. Her relationships have been covered in tabloids, mocking her for teenage love. This has served as inspiration for her and an eventual middle finger to anyone who wrongly broke her heart. Since her teenagers, Swift has been involved publicly in relationships constantly. All which became public interest. This culminated in what may be her dark opus covering celebrity breakups and media coverage of their relationships. In recent years she has begun to recapture some control over how she portrays herself publicly, through an app that offers exclusive content and music. Multiple opinion and taste studies argue the app is making fans like Swift more than they did before, which options for a mobile match game that rewards fans for incorporating Swift's songs into their playlists.

Charitable Work and Philanthropic Efforts

Swift has demonstrated a commitment to various causes and initiatives, and regularly leverages her substantial platform as part of this work. While many celebrities work with larger nonprofit organizations, or even create their own, in order to provide financial backing to a range of causes, Swift's efforts have often been more personally hands-on. The following section highlights both Swift's philanthropy and efforts to directly support charitable initiatives.

Support for charitable work and philanthropy is often demonstrated by an individual's financial contributions to a cause, as facilitated by large or small donations. Yet celebrities also raise awareness and express their support for various causes in any number of ways, including through social media campaigns, videos, and by making public appearances at benefit events. Indeed, some well-known names use their status to found and fund individual philanthropic organizations or foundations that contribute widely to other established charities, as opposed to focusing solely on a single cause. Taylor Swift is known for her personal involvement in a range of different charitable and philanthropic organizations. Some, such as the Red Cross, The National Resources Defense Council and The United Nations High Commissioner for Refugees, encompass a variety of different causes and support a diverse array of projects. Others, such as The V Foundation for Cancer Research, focus on a single issue, and are more wholeheartedly dedicated to providing financial support. In every instance, supporting options such as those listed under this heading offers assistance to an already-established charity that remains in need of ongoing financial support from the public.

CHAPTER 11

Conclusion: Taylor Swift's Enduring Legacy and Fut

In so many ways, Taylor Swift's success story is one of a kind – unique in ways that cannot be artificially recreated the same way a new artist can mimic or copy another one. In this book, I've outlined dozens of elements or experiences that can perhaps only ever happen once, with one specific artist at one particular time and place in history: from her humble beginnings in rural Wyomissing, Pennsylvania, to her father's Christmas-Tree-farm-financed Nashville demo recording sessions, to being the MySpace phenomenon, to being Eddie Vedder's opening act, to rapping with T Pain (or not rapping at all); while original in her own right, to what extent will Swift's legacy remain perhaps nothing more than an unsuccessful pop star? Given all that I've chronicled here – and I may have even missed some things! – just how lasting of an impact has Swift already made? Can a "flash-in-the-pan" pop artist really be expected to have a tremendous impact more than a decade after she finally did break into the mainstream pop world with her first documented "pop zombie"? After fifteen years, how many acts other than Adele, who operates on a similar World-Stage stardom level, even have had a platform to accomplish what this tireless svengali to the biz music enthusiast finally has?

Of course, these questions and others remain to be seen. However, it is my conclusion that the exclusive, nineteen-record recording contract Taylor Swift signed and negotiated (and/or renegotiated as she deemed necessary) with Universal Records (and the recorded product it contains) is indeed the key to understanding her legacy fifty years from now, as it frees her from the pressure of topping the music business mammoths of yesteryear. In writing this book, I mostly have only been able to speculate about the long-term impact of Swift's career thus far. However, Taylor Swift's and Adele's multiple 11,000,000 album- and single-sales may suggest the way in which Swift (and perhaps Adele too) may yet have a future impact on the music and entertainment industry in the years, perhaps long into the future.